Bible Reade

A Study of Romans

GOOD NEWS
FOR
GOD'S PEOPLE

William Carter

Abingdon Press / Nashville

GOOD NEWS FOR GOD'S PEOPLE
A STUDY OF ROMANS

Scripture quotations in this publication, unless otherwise indicated, are from the New Revised Standard Version of the Bible, copyrighted © 1989 by the Division of Christian Education of the National Council of the Churches of Christ in the United States of America, and are used by permission.

Lessons are based on the International Sunday School Lessons for Christian Teaching, copyright © 1990, by the Committee on the Uniform Series. Text excerpted from *Adult Bible Studies,* Spring 1994.

ISBN 0-687-08218-8

06 07 08 09—10 9 8 7
Manufactured in the United States of America.

CONTENTS

Chapter One

SAVED BY FAITH

PURPOSE

To affirm that through faith we participate in God's salvation

BIBLE PASSAGE

Romans 1:1, 3-17

1 Paul, a servant of Jesus Christ, called to be an apostle, set apart for the gospel of God . . . 3 the gospel concerning his Son, who was descended from David according to the flesh 4 and was declared to be Son of God with power according to the spirit of holiness by resurrection from the dead, Jesus Christ our Lord, 5 through whom we have received grace and apostleship to bring about the obedience of faith among all the Gentiles for the sake of his name, 6 including yourselves who are called to belong to Jesus Christ,

7 To all God's beloved in Rome, who are called to be saints:

Grace to you and peace from God our Father and the Lord Jesus Christ.

8 First, I thank my God through Jesus Christ for all of you, because your faith is proclaimed throughout the world.

9 **For God, whom I serve with my spirit by announcing the gospel of his Son, is my witness that without ceasing I remember you always in my prayers,** 10 **asking that by God's will I may somehow at last succeed in coming to you.** 11 **For I am longing to see you so that I may share with you some spiritual gift to strengthen you—** 12 **or rather so that we may be mutually encouraged by each other's faith, both yours and mine.** 13 **I want you to know, brothers and sisters, that I have often intended to come to you (but thus far have been prevented), in order that I may reap some harvest among you as I have among the rest of the Gentiles.** 14 **I am a debtor both to Greeks and to barbarians, both to the wise and to the foolish** 15 **—hence my eagerness to proclaim the gospel to you also who are in Rome.**

16 **For I am not ashamed of the gospel; it is the power of God for salvation to everyone who has faith, to the Jew first and also to the Greek.** 17 **For in it the righteousness of God is revealed through faith for faith; as it is written, "The one who is righteous will live by faith."**

CORE VERSE

I am not ashamed of the gospel; it is the power of God for salvation to everyone who has faith, to the Jew first and also to the Greek.   *(Romans 1:16)*

OUR NEED

Since Dan was the youngest boy in our family, my brother Jim and I tended to tease him a great deal. For instance, we would sometimes place him on the porch of the house, about four feet high, and stand on the ground, urging him to jump into our arms. He adamantly refused to do so, no matter how much we cajoled or threatened. But when our father stood on the same spot and told him to jump, Dan would hurl himself into the air enthusiastically, with absolute confidence that he would be safely caught and hugged.

It was only later that Jim and I realized that we had put Dan in some danger. Then we understood the measure of trust that he displayed in our father's love.

Christians go through a similar process when we put aside our inhibitions and throw ourselves on the mercies of God, believing that we can trust God to love us and save us. Through faith we discover the power of God's saving love.

FAITHFUL LIVING

Paul had preached the gospel throughout Asia Minor and Greece. Although Gentiles were the major focus of his ministry, Paul found early on that people acquainted with what we call the Old Testament and with the traditions of Israel were those most likely to respond to his message. For this reason he often sought out the synagogue when he came to a new place.

Many of those who embraced his teaching were "God-fearers," Gentiles who accepted the theology but not the practice of Judaism. Some Jewish Christians felt it was necessary for those Gentiles who entered the faith to observe all the customs of Israel before they could become full Christians. Those practices included abstinence from certain types of meat; the observance of specific festival days; and keeping the laws regarding religious behavior, worship, and other aspects of Jewish community life, including the rite of circumcision as the symbol of membership.

Paul seems to have fought strongly against this tendency to "Judaize" the gospel. His disagreement was not with Judaism as such but with those who argued that Gentiles must assume all the obligations of the Mosaic law. Paul's letters, especially the one to Galatia, strongly emphasized that these laws and traditions were of no use to the new faith because it was founded entirely on Jesus Christ, who had both fulfilled and superseded the old law. Faith in Jesus Christ as Savior was the key to salvation.

The concept of justification—that is, being right with God—by faith alone was at the center of Paul's understanding of the gospel. Many Christians in Asia Minor and Greece accepted this doctrine, but some in Jerusalem were uneasy with Paul's message. So he had collected contributions for the struggling Jerusalem church from his mostly Gentile congregations to help ease concerns and to demonstrate the unity of the church.

At the point of going to Jerusalem with his collection, Paul wrote from Corinth to the church at Rome. Rome was a cosmopolitan city, and the Christian church there contained both Jews and Gentiles. Inspired by God, Paul reviewed many of the central tenets of his teaching. He hoped that the church in the capital city would understand his message and support it, both in his relations with Jerusalem and in his future missionary endeavors.

Paul's Credentials

It is easy for us to forget that for many early Christians, Paul was just another traveling missionary. While the eleven original apostles had a clear relationship to Jesus (and the new twelfth apostle, Matthias, had been selected by them; Acts 1:15-26), it was not always apparent how other early teachers and preachers gained their authority. Stephen and six others had been appointed by the apostles for special work (Acts 6:1-6), and Barnabas had been sent by the Twelve to serve as pastor of the new congregation at Antioch (Acts 11:19-26). Paul was a wild card, not altogether trusted by the "establishment."

In fact, there is evidence that Paul and Peter had more than one confrontation; and Paul was very careful to declare his independence from the Jerusalem group in his letter to the Galatians (1:11–2:14). Although we know Paul as one through whom the Lord worked to take the new faith throughout the Roman world, many in his own time first saw him as a threat to theological purity.

For that reason, Paul was always careful to speak of his own experience of selection as an "apostle" whenever he addressed a new group. Since many of those at Rome knew him already (Romans 16:1-16), he provides only a quick summary; but it is filled with meaning.

Paul calls himself a "servant of Jesus Christ" (Romans 1:1), with all that such a relationship implies. That is, he is not his own master; his actions are directed by the one who owns his labor; and what he says reflects the will of the one for whom he works.

Paul tells his readers that he was "called to be an apostle" (Romans 1:1). While he cannot claim membership in the original group who walked with the earthly Jesus, Paul's spiritual experience is so intense that he is certain that God has called him to proclaim the "gospel concerning his son" (Romans 1:3). Since there must have been many persons claiming such authority, we can assume that Paul's testimony was especially impressive; for the early church accepted his writings as inspired.

Furthermore, Paul asserts that he has been "set apart for the gospel of God . . . to bring about the obedience of faith among all the Gentiles for the sake of his name, including yourselves" (Romans 1:1, 5-6). Paul has a special call, one that sets him apart from the other apostles: to proclaim the good news to the Gentiles. (Note: Peter is reported to have received a similar call; see Acts 15:6-8.)

Not only do Paul's credentials qualify him for the ministry of the word, he has a special responsibility and authority for the very persons to whom he addresses the letter.

We cannot overestimate how important this step was in the history of the faith. If Paul had not managed to establish himself as God's messenger for the Gentiles, the followers of Jesus may well have become a minor Jewish sect. Instead, Christianity blossomed into an expression of faith among people throughout the world. The Letter to Rome played no small part in that transformation.

What are some of your credentials for witnessing to the faith?

Laying the Groundwork

Once Paul has established his authority, he immediately moves to gain the confidence of the Roman Christians. To those among us who feel that courtesy and good interpersonal relationships are of minimal importance in the proclamation of the gospel, he provides a valuable lesson.

Paul tells the Roman Christians, "I thank my God through Jesus Christ for all of you, because your faith is proclaimed throughout the world" (Romans 1:8). While we know that Paul will set forth his own theological position, he does not attack his readers' theology. Perhaps that was a lesson he had learned with the Christians of Corinth, where he did attack; apparently, he never resolved the problems there (see the letters to Corinth, especially the second one, Chapters 10–13).

Now Paul sets a pattern that could become a model for Christian communication everywhere. He commends the Romans' faith, even though he knows that it may not reflect completely his own understanding of the fullness of the gospel. He follows that with the assurance that they are always in his prayers. Acceptance and prayer for each other is much better than fulmination (getting hot under the collar), whatever the circumstances.

Paul expresses a desire to be in the Romans' presence, to share some "spiritual gift" (Romans 1:11) with them for their benefit. Then recognizing that he may sound a little condescending, Paul changes the phrase to state the hope that he and they may be "mutually encouraged" (Romans 1:12). Here is an example of a skill we may not have known Paul had: He knew how to make people aware that their feelings were important to him.

Such consideration is a vital part of conversations between Christians, especially when they know they differ from one another. If we do not make known our love and respect for one another, who will?

Finally, Paul declares himself to be a debtor "both to Greeks and to barbarians, both to the wise and to the foolish" (Romans 1:14). He does not want to appear arrogant or superior. Rather, he reveals his own dependence on many sources of understanding and hopes that others will be open as well.

While Paul has confidence in his own faith, he often warns against spiritual pride and judgments about the motives of others (Romans 12:3; Philippians 1:15-18). In fact, he even asserts his own intention of being adaptable to persons everywhere so that they will be more inclined to receive the good news (1 Corinthians 9:19-23).

The groundwork has been laid. Paul has reassured the people that he is on their side, that he cares for them, and that he is aware they share a great desire to know the faith. Now he is ready to begin the teaching that will provide deeper understanding for all.

What kinds of things do you do to prepare for a discussion that may involve points of conflict?

Setting the Record Straight

Paul was deeply concerned about righteousness. For a Jew, righteousness (being in right relation to God) was the chief objective of life. Thus the focus of much Hebrew religious thought was on the process by which righteousness could be obtained.

During the periods before and after the prophets, some strands of Judaism concentrated on the observance of the laws regarding religious and personal behavior as the way to ensure that persons would be made righteous or justified. Those who were justified were saved. That is, they escaped the wages of sin; and their life became one with God.

Led by the Holy Spirit in his reading of the Hebrew Scriptures, Paul saw that the writings did not uniformly support the idea that law was the primary source of justification. He knew from his own experience that faith rather than works was the avenue of access to God's salvation. But Paul did not want to dismiss the wisdom of hundreds of years of Hebrew religion. It was very important to him and to the future of the faith that there be no contradiction between the old covenant and the new. After all, the concept of the Messiah was rooted in Judaism; and that was an idea he could build upon.

Because Paul was both a well-trained scholar and a person who listened to God, he found a number of passages in the Hebrew Scriptures, especially in the writings of the prophets, demonstrating that true righteousness came through faith—as made clear through the gospel of Jesus Christ. Paul set out to help the Romans understand this theological insight.

What are some of the insights about your faith that came to you through reading the Old Testament?

The Righteous Live by Faith

Paul expresses confidence in the gospel: "It is the power of God for salvation to everyone who has faith. . . . For in it the righteousness of God is revealed through faith for faith" (Romans 1:16-17).

In this eloquent passage Paul states the role of faith in the process of justification. Only through faith do we discover the love of God, the source of our salvation. Faith brings us into contact with the power of the gospel. It is the field into which the grace of God can descend to prepare the mind and heart for the greater glories of faith that grace can finally bring—by faith for faith.

Salvation is from God, by his grace alone. We have done nothing to deserve it, and we can do nothing to guarantee it. Our faith enables us to participate in God's salvation; we are justified by God's grace as we believe God's word.

When Paul quotes the phrase from Habakkuk 2:4, "The one who is righteous will live by faith" (Romans 1:17), he means to tie the concept of salvation by faith firmly to its Old Testament roots. The prophets understood it that way; surely, their descendants can do no less.

In what ways does faith prepare us to receive God's grace?

Through Faith to Faithfulness

In a gentle way, Paul has begun his task of making sure that the Romans understand the faith/salvation process. He will later argue the case from many perspectives, but at this point he has really said all he needs to say to establish his point. Faith is the source of our response to God's act in salvation through grace. When we experience faith in Jesus Christ, we discover the power of God's saving love.

CLOSING PRAYER
God, cure our unbelief, that we may share your salvation. In the name of your Son we pray. Amen.

Chapter Two

RECEIVING GOD'S GIFT

PURPOSE

To help us recognize that in response to God's grace, faith in Christ has priority over obedience to the law

BIBLE PASSAGE

Romans 4:13-25

13 **For the promise that he would inherit the world did not come to Abraham or to his descendants through the law but through the righteousness of faith.** 14 **If it is the adherents of the law who are to be the heirs, faith is null and the promise is void.** 15 **For the law brings wrath; but where there is no law, neither is there violation.**

16 **For this reason it depends on faith, in order that the promise may rest on grace and be guaranteed to all his descendants, not only to the adherents of the law but also to those who share the faith of Abraham (for he is the father of all of us,** 17 **as it is written, "I have made you the father of many nations")—in the presence of the God in whom he believed, who gives life to the dead and calls into existence the things that do not exist.** 18 **Hoping against hope, he believed that he would become "the father of many nations," according to what was said, "So numerous shall your descendants be."** 19 **He**

did not weaken in faith when he considered his own body, which was already as good as dead (for he was about a hundred years old), or when he considered the barrenness of Sarah's womb. 20 No distrust made him waver concerning the promise of God, but he grew strong in his faith as he gave glory to God, 21 being fully convinced that God was able to do what he had promised. 22 Therefore his faith "was reckoned to him as righteousness." 23 Now the words, "it was reckoned to him," were written not for his sake alone, 24 but for ours also. It will be reckoned to us who believe in him who raised Jesus our Lord from the dead, 25 who was handed over to death for our trespasses and was raised for our justification.

CORE VERSE

The promise that he would inherit the world did not come to Abraham or to his descendants through the law but through the righteousness of faith. *(Romans 4:13)*

OUR NEED

Between worship services in The Unicoi United Methodist Church, where I had been invited to preach, I attended a Sunday school class taught by a former pastor. It was a delightful experience. The class was friendly, the teacher was prepared, and the lesson was interesting.

In making a point about faith, Joe referred to the story of the death of Lazarus in John 11. When Jesus met Martha outside the town of Bethany, she was distraught. Her anguish caused her to accuse Jesus of neglecting his good friend Lazarus, allowing him to die. Jesus replied that Lazarus would rise again, but Martha was not ready to believe that her brother's resurrection would take place soon.

So Jesus asked her if she believed in his power to ensure eternal life. She seemed to avoid a direct answer, but her reply went beyond the question: "Lord, I believe that you are the

Messiah" (John 11:27). As the teacher put it, "She didn't know whether she believed he could raise Lazarus, but she knew that she believed in Jesus."

It is just that kind of faith that triumphs over death. We do not really know everything about the law or about grace, but we do believe in Jesus. As we are reminded in our Bible passage, that is the most important thing. For faith in God's grace expressed in the life, teaching, death, and resurrection of Jesus Christ brings salvation. Just as he was "raised for our justification" (Romans 4:25), we will be raised through the mercy of God—not through our keeping the law or our having the right opinions.

FAITHFUL LIVING

At the time of Paul's letter to the Romans, most Christians were immersed in the Scriptures of the people of Israel. These early believers knew the Hebrew Bible as the authentic Word of God. Thus whatever teachings could not be supported by the Old Testament tradition had little chance of acceptance in the Christian community.

In the stories and traditions of the people of Israel, no person was more important than Abraham. He was not only the revered ancestor, he was the one through whom the idea of the nation itself was transmitted. The "children of Abraham" were heirs to a vision that had brought their forefather and his family from Ur in the Chaldees to the land of promise. Thus for Jews any proposed revision in the traditional understanding of personal or national aspirations was subject to the test of conformity with God's word to Abraham.

While the patriarch was not the giver of the law, it was assumed that the law was a result of the steadfast presence of God in Abraham's life and in the early years of the formation of the people of Israel. Paul's inspired decision to develop an alternative view of Abraham's contribution to the life and faith of the nation was one of his own contributions to the early Christian church. By using the Scripture as his source, he established in one stroke the continuity of God's reign and the authority of the concept of justification by faith. Through Paul's writing and teaching, the Word spoke to a new generation in a new way.

In what ways do you find God revealed in the Old Testament? What additional insights does the New Testament bring to your understanding?

Abraham, Our Father

Throughout Romans 2 and 3, Paul carefully builds his argument against the use of adherence to the law as the standard by which to achieve acceptance by God. Paul also warns about using such a standard to judge others (Romans 2:1-11). Circumcision, a crucial issue in the controversy over true righteousness, is examined briefly (Romans 2:25–3:4); and the conclusion is that "real circumcision is a matter of the heart" (Romans 2:29). In Chapter 3, Paul comments that all have fallen short of righteousness, even those who keep the law. Therefore circumcised and uncircumcised will be justified by the same thing: faith.

It is here that Paul inserts an observation from the Hebrew Scriptures to support the idea that faith is the ground of all relationships with God. "Abraham believed God, and it was reckoned to him as righteousness" (Romans 4:3). This citation of Genesis 15:6 takes the discussion of the law versus grace/faith back to the time before the law existed, pointing out that faith or trust came first. Then Paul follows with the statement that begins our Bible passage: "For the promise that he would inherit the world did not come to Abraham or to his descendants through the law but through the righteousness of faith" (Romans 4:13).

It is absolutely necessary, Paul maintains, that the promise rest on faith because otherwise there would be no access to grace for anyone and no justification for those who were reared outside the law. However, if we examine the scriptural account, we can see that the initiation of the promise to Abraham was through faith. That made God's grace available to all descendants of Abraham, which includes people of many nations, not just the Jews; for Abraham was "the father of all of us" (Romans 4:16)—Jewish Christians and Gentile Christians (Romans 4:11-12).

Clearly, faith is much more important than the works of the law and always has been. But now there is both new meaning and new promise for all through Jesus Christ, "who was handed over to death for our trespasses and was raised for our justification" (Romans 4:25). The time has come to recognize that the promise to Abraham has finally been realized. Faith has become the ground of our hope.

How does the realization that all believers are of one ancestry affect your appreciation of other members of the wider community of faith?

Law and Grace

Since there are no actions we can perform or rituals we can follow that will influence God to declare us righteous, what hope do we have? If works are useless and religious activities are of no avail, what can we do? Paul proclaims that we can believe that God's grace will be sufficient for our needs. Moreover, God has already prepared the way for access to that grace through the death of Jesus on the cross. All we have to do to receive it is to have faith.

This is the "free gift" that replaces the works righteousness of the law. The law Paul refers to is the law of the religious community. For Jews in Paul's day, this law gave instructions on how and when to prepare sacrifices, ordered relationships between people, described rituals to be used in public and private worship, and prohibited certain individual and group activities. This law was held in high esteem, even by Paul. But the apostle argues that such law is not the means of justification before God.

Paul is careful to say that the adherents of the law have access to this free gift of God's grace; after all, he had experienced it in his own life. But all men and women, Jew and Gentile alike, must come to God through Christ. "It depends on faith, in order that the promise may rest on grace and be guaranteed to all his [Abraham's] descendants" (Romans 4:16).

Neither the Hebrew law nor any other set of legal definitions can determine what God will do for people. That is a matter for grace alone; and grace flows from the very nature of God, which is love.

Receiving the gift means that we have passed from death to life. Spirit has replaced flesh. A new creature has been created— with a new set of joys and a new understanding of life. The relationship to God has been adjusted by God, not by us; and the future no longer seems bleak and unpromising.

However, the replacement of the works of the law by faith does not mean that we are free from all restraints on behavior or from the urgencies of our bodies and the vagaries of our minds. There is still a considerable battle to be fought.

In another part of Romans, Paul calls the law and the commandments "holy" and "spiritual" (Romans 7:12, 14). While the law of the religious community will not save us, there is nothing inherently evil about it. It is the law of the inner self, the law of sin, that is truly destructive. It is this force that we must constantly guard against and bring under control (Romans 12:9-21). As Paul said in his letter to the Philippians, we must "work out [our] own salvation with fear and trembling" (Philippians 2:12).

Thus our freedom from the law does not mean freedom from responsibility. God is still God, and the laws of the universe and the moral life are fixed. While we may not yet understand all of them and certainly do not understand some of them, they are there as a part of a creation that took place long before we were born.

Acting against these laws will have serious consequences, but these consequences do not need to be devastating. Accepting the gift of God in faith means not only knowing that God's grace will justify us but also that God will be with us in our successes and in our failures.

What questions do you have about physical and moral laws? How does God help you cope with your questions?

Strengthening the Church

The leaders of the Protestant Reformation considered the Letter to the Romans one of the most important writings in the New Testament. There are several reasons we would attest to the accuracy of that judgment.

First, the fact that the presentation was made to the church at Rome was crucial. As the capital of the Empire, Rome was an influential center. Even though the Empire was long hostile toward the new faith and many civil and military leaders were prepared to attack Christians at the slightest provocation, Rome remained the seat of power for many years. Therefore many opportunities existed to communicate with those who held the temporal destiny of nations and peoples in their hands. The beliefs of the Roman Christians would be shared with many others, some of whom could affect the course of history. The emphasis on faith rather than on works made the Christian religion distinctive and engaging.

Second, Paul's interpretation of Scripture in Romans also made it possible for more of the Jewish population to feel comfortable in the new faith. Some who joined early were lost when it became apparent that Jesus was not the kind of Messiah they had expected. Paul's writing provided a rationale for the difference while explaining the continuity between the new and old covenants. Many persons of tender conscience needed this understanding to remain true to their commitment to follow Christ.

Christianity gradually became a largely Gentile movement; fewer and fewer of Abraham's physical descendants came into the group as time went on. But the church would not have survived without those faithful persons who brought their Hebrew faith to form the foundation for the new covenant. The Letter to the Galatians had made many of the same points, but it sounded to some like an attack on the law as such. The Letter to the Romans said similar things in a way that healed wounds and made friends.

Finally, the letter gave a fresh start to those Gentiles who were still wondering if the new faith had anything to offer them. Most of the non-Jewish religions of the day were centered around some mythical figure who represented escape from the world and offered a form of worship that bore almost no relationship to moral living or to personal restraints of any kind.

By contrast, Christianity was demanding and promised few earthly advantages. In fact, the cross was its visible symbol. Who would choose such a cause?

Who? Precisely those who wanted a new life. That life was bought with a price but given freely by God to those who received it in faith. That extraordinary grace promised a life eternal, guaranteed by the resurrection of the one who had died for all.

This was a faith people could embrace, a faith people could die for. With the old legalism swept away and trust in God made the dominant theme in the process of salvation, it was now possible for all people to enjoy the beatitude of God. With their father, Abraham, they could all "inherit the world" and the world to come—and so can we!

How does Paul's message of salvation by grace help you in your efforts to bring the love of Christ to people in our time?

CLOSING PRAYER
God of the Hebrew, God of the Roman, God of the people of the world, renew in us the faith that will enable us to receive daily the grace to be made whole and to offer wholeness to others. In Jesus' name we pray. Amen.

Chapter Three

BEING RECONCILED TO GOD

PURPOSE

To help increase our understanding of the meaning of justification and reconciliation in Christ

BIBLE PASSAGE

Romans 5:6-17

6 For while we were still weak, at the right time Christ died for the ungodly. 7 Indeed, rarely will anyone die for a righteous person—though perhaps for a good person someone might actually dare to die. 8 But God proves his love for us in that while we still were sinners Christ died for us. 9 Much more surely then, now that we have been justified by his blood, will we be saved through him from the wrath of God. 10 For if while we were enemies, we were reconciled to God through the death of his Son, much more surely, having been reconciled, will we be saved by his life. 11 But more than that, we even boast in God through our Lord Jesus Christ, through whom we have now received reconciliation.

12 Therefore, just as sin came into the world through one man, and death came through sin, and so death spread to all because all have sinned— 13 sin was indeed in the world

before the law, but sin is not reckoned when there is no law. 14 Yet death exercised dominion from Adam to Moses, even over those whose sins were not like the transgression of Adam, who is a type of the one who was to come.

15 But the free gift is not like the trespass. For if the many died through the one man's trespass, much more surely have the grace of God and the free gift in the grace of the one man, Jesus Christ, abounded for the many. 16 And the free gift is not like the effect of the one man's sin. For the judgment following one trespass brought condemnation, but the free gift following many trespasses brings justification. 17 If, because of the one man's trespass, death exercised dominion through that one, much more surely will those who receive the abundance of grace and the free gift of righteousness exercise dominion in life through the one man, Jesus Christ.

CORE VERSE

God proves his love for us in that while we still were sinners Christ died for us.   *(Romans 5:8)*

OUR NEED

In one of the churches I served, there were two persons, neighbors, who had fallen into hostility over a trivial matter many years earlier. Both of them continued to attend church and participated in community events, but they did not speak to each other. Many times they would be in the same conversational group, but each acted as though the other were not present. They had been that way so long that everyone assumed they would never change. But they did. During a spiritual enrichment weekend, they were almost simultaneously struck with the absurdity of their relationship. They even made a public confession of their sin and announced their intention to put the whole matter behind them. To nearly everyone's surprise, they became fast friends and spent the rest of their lives as true neighbors.

That memory has been for me a symbol of the meaning of reconciliation. Recently, I read a definition of the word from a book I have saved from my school days: "Reconciliation has the significance of a new stage in personal relationships in which previous hostility of mind or estrangement has been put away in some decisive act."[1] Certainly, that is what happened to those good friends.

Paul tells us that a similar thing happens to those who come to know Jesus Christ. We are all estranged from God by a wide gulf of our own making. This distance is not bridgeable by ordinary means. But through Jesus Christ reconciliation is possible, and life can be lived in a new dimension. That is what the gospel is all about.

FAITHFUL LIVING

Romans 5 begins with the words, "Therefore, since we are justified by faith," words that lead us to expect we are going to learn what happens when persons receive the grace of God. That expectation will not be disappointed.

The first result is "peace with God" (Romans 5:1). Whatever sort of life we have lived, we never possess the peace that passes understanding until we know that God has accepted us as we are and has made us righteous. That peace is the consequence of grace.

Access to grace is through Jesus Christ. The life of Jesus and his death on the cross have opened the eyes of those who will see God as God really is. In this new light the truth of God produces contentment of the spirit. That contentment is what we mean by peace. Peace brings not the absence of conflict but the presence of assurance. Being assured that God views us as righteous because of Jesus Christ frees us to deal with the everyday trials of life.

Also, justification brings "hope of sharing the glory of

God" (Romans 5:2). While we do not (and cannot) know the fullness of the glory of God, we can expect to be full participants in it as it is revealed. In both this life and the life to come, there are glorious moments with God that those who have been justified will share. The joy of salvation is not to be deferred; it is part of the present as well as part of the future. There is a continuity here. As suggested by the title of a devotional work by Henry Scougal, it is a "life of God in the soul of man."

How have you experienced peace and glory in your Christian life?

The Ladder Up From Suffering

In a sudden shift of mood, Paul even includes pride in suffering as one of the benefits of justification. Instead of something to be ashamed of, suffering is seen as a cause to boast (Romans 5:3).

Of course, Paul does not mean that we should be proud of the suffering we experience because of our mistakes or because of life's misfortunes. (However, even that kind of suffering may provide strength in the long run.) What he is talking about is the suffering that persons endure because of their faith.

In our time we have heard much about the advantages of faith. We have been promised many rewards (such as health, wealth, and happiness) by those who want our contributions to their ministries. So it is easy to forget that the faith itself often brings suffering. It certainly did in the first century. We can assume that there were many during that time who wondered why they were suffering instead of gaining, just as there are many today. Paul tries to reassure them.

Suffering, he says, is one of the foundations of strong faith. It produces endurance, which is a source of character. Character might be defined as the inner moral strength that underlies hope. The hope that comes from false expectations or bravado may not be realized, but the hope of faith always is. It is based on trust in the wisdom and mercy of God rather than on the desire for a more comfortable life.

Christian hope is empowered by the love of God that has been poured into our hearts. It is the way upward from suffering, like a ladder out of a crater, leading to a safe summit. It is the crest of God's love, which encourages and sustains us.

The life described above is the fruit of justification, which comes as a gift from God through Jesus Christ. His death opens the way for our restoration to full fellowship with God.

What are the true objectives of Christian hope? How do we reach them?

While We Were Sinners

Once there was considerable interest in the concept of "positive reinforcement," based on the work of B. F. Skinner. The theory is that persons are more likely to change their behavior if their good actions are rewarded than if their bad actions are punished. Some research seemed to indicate that such reinforcement does work. As a result, many persons used the method in the classroom and in the workplace.

Of course, a large group of people disagreed. They said that discipline, including immediate punishment for unacceptable behavior, is the only way people can be restrained from destructive action. These thinkers advocated a more restrictive plan with specific rules and punishments.

The amazing thing about the gospel is that it does not support either approach. What it says is that "while we still were sinners Christ died for us" (Romans 5:8). We are neither rewarded for past good behavior nor punished for past bad behavior. Instead, God takes charge of the process and directly intervenes to open the way for release from sin. The only condition is acceptance of this great gift.

Instead of rewards and punishments, the gospel is about grace. The whole sacrificial system of repeated acts of atonement is set aside. It is replaced by the grace of God expressed in Jesus Christ. God does not wait for us to cleanse ourselves; we are forgiven because God loves us, not because we have done anything to deserve it. Justification is thus realized by faith in Christ alone—and not by any actions we perform or omit.

In some of his letters Paul acknowledges that many persons in the early church could not accept this doctrine (1 Corinthians 1:18-31; Galatians 3:1-14). We still have some problems with it in our time, for often we talk about grace but practice some form of reward and punishment. We find it very hard to believe that God restores the sinner without exacting a price. We can hardly believe that it is true for us; and it may be even more difficult to accept that God offers the same opportunity to everyone, even the worst offender. But God does. We are all justified by God's act in Christ while we are still sinners.

Are you comfortable with the interpretation of justification by faith given above? If not, what would you change?

While We Were Enemies

Paul also maintains that justification takes place even in the midst of our alienation and hostility—even though we may be enemies of God and of one another. This too may be hard to accept.

When there is a true change of heart, however, there is a corresponding change in relationships. Genuine love is the only way to reach enduring solutions at any level. The embrace of the two persons who found a way out of their dilemma, noted in our opening section, is a model of what happens on any level when reconciliation occurs. Enemies are changed into friends (reconciled) when love replaces fear and distrust.

That is exactly what God did for humankind. Human beings have an opposition, a resistance to God. We are estranged from God, not God from us. Paul speaks of our need for reconciliation, not God's. But God effects this reconciliation, not as a product of a series of problem-solving steps, but as the result of an extraordinary outpouring of love. Despite human fear and misunderstanding, God reveals in Jesus Christ that love is the foundation of all relations between God and humankind.

That same love enables us to achieve reconciliation with and among our fellow human beings. Even the most persistent enemy responds to undemanding love. Although we sometimes doubt it and fear that we will be taken advantage of, we know that it is true. The only way we humans will ever achieve peace with one another is through the expression of an unconditional love rooted in that of God, who, while we were enemies of God, revealed such love through Jesus.

How has God's reconciling love for you affected your relationships with other people?

Reconciliation Is Real

At this point a short review of history may be helpful.

The Protestant Reformation was born as a reaction against the idea that overcoming sin was a matter of performing penances or obtaining indulgences from the church. Using the Bible and especially the letters of Paul as his source, Martin Luther declared that justification was realized by faith in Jesus Christ; no actions of individuals or of the church had any effect. God's grace was the source of salvation.

It was an inspired idea. Many of the Protestants in the

world today trace back their existence to Luther's perception and to his persistence in the face of great opposition.

But these early Protestants did not follow up with a clear affirmation of the relationship of reconciliation to the primary doctrine of justification. Only in recent years has that theme emerged as a basic expression of the faith. It may be that the New Testament is so rich in theological and moral insight that each generation discovers something not seen before.

The growing conviction that justification and the accompanying reconciliation to God have profound implications for relationships between people is also rooted in Scripture. When Paul writes that "while we were enemies, we were reconciled to God" (Romans 5:10), he means not only enemies of God but also enemies of one another. In Romans 2, he clearly identifies separation between Jews and the new Gentile Christians as one of the great stumbling blocks to faith. In the Galatian letter he crowns his discussion of grace and justification with the statement that "there is no longer Jew or Greek, there is no longer slave or free, there is no longer male and female; for all of you are one in Christ Jesus" (Galatians 3:28). The reconciling act of God affects all our relationships.

Furthermore, reconciliation becomes a part of our own ministry. In 2 Corinthians 5:18, there is a positive statement: "All this is from God, who reconciled us to himself through Christ, and has given us the ministry of reconciliation." That ministry includes both sharing the message that men and women may be reconciled to God and spreading the truth that when God accepts us as his children, we all become brothers and sisters in Christ (2 Corinthians 5:18-20). Part of the task of the Christian is to make sure that every person knows that loving God also involves loving others.

We are both the reconciled and the reconcilers. When Christians concentrate on finding the things that divide us and spend most of our time attacking other believers, we lose the essence of the faith, which is that the love of God and the love of others are both part of the same good news. The love of God and the love of humankind cannot be separated if faith is to have integrity.

Paul concluded this section of his letter to the Romans with a statement of the abundance of grace that God offers to those who will receive him. The trespass that separated all persons from God brought condemnation through the action of one person (Adam). The free gift brings justification and reconciliation to all persons—without regard to ancestry, previous religious practice, gender, or position in society—through the action of one person (Jesus). While Christians are still struggling to live up to Christ's ideal in our personal and social lives, it is the foundation on which the faith is built, the goal to which Christian action is directed.

This abundant grace of God is the greatest resource any of us has. How could we live without it? Yet at times we seem to feel that grace is something we own and something those of whom we disapprove must live without. After all, how can God act to overcome their estrangement? But God does. For all people. Even our enemies. Even God's enemies. Reconciliation is real.

[1] From *A Theological Word Book of the Bible,* edited by Alan Richardson (The Macmillan Company, 1950); page 185.

CLOSING PRAYER
God of all, give us hearts to accept others and to seek the joys of reconciliation everywhere. In the name of Jesus Christ, our Lord, we pray. Amen.

Chapter Four

DELIVERED FROM SIN

PURPOSE

To help us consider how God's grace frees us to say no to old ways and yes to new life in Christ

BIBLE PASSAGE

Romans 6:3-14, 20-23

3 Do you not know that all of us who have been baptized into Christ Jesus were baptized into his death? 4 Therefore we have been buried with him by baptism into death, so that, just as Christ was raised from the dead by the glory of the Father, so we too might walk in newness of life.

5 For if we have been united with him in a death like his, we will certainly be united with him in a resurrection like his. 6 We know that our old self was crucified with him so that the body of sin might be destroyed, and we might no longer be enslaved to sin. 7 For whoever has died is freed from sin. 8 But if we have died with Christ, we believe that we will also live with him. 9 We know that Christ, being raised from the dead, will never die again; death no longer has dominion over him. 10 The death he died, he died to sin, once for all; but the life he lives, he lives to God. 11 So you also must consider yourselves dead to sin and alive to God in Christ Jesus.

12 Therefore, do not let sin exercise dominion in your mortal bodies, to make you obey their passions. 13 No longer present your members to sin as instruments of wickedness, but present yourselves to God as those who have been brought from death to life, and present your members to God as instruments of righteousness. 14 For sin will have no dominion over you, since you are not under law but under grace. . . .

20 When you were slaves of sin, you were free in regard to righteousness. 21 So what advantage did you then get from the things of which you now are ashamed? The end of those things is death. 22 But now that you have been freed from sin and enslaved to God, the advantage you get is sanctification. The end is eternal life. 23 For the wages of sin is death, but the free gift of God is eternal life in Christ Jesus our Lord.

CORE VERSE

The wages of sin is death, but the free gift of God is eternal life in Christ Jesus our Lord. *(Romans 6:23)*

OUR NEED

Some years ago I wrote a series of lessons on the Gospel of John. In the text I made a statement that being a Christian involves more than verbal commitment—that God expects us to act the faith as well as to claim it. A few days after publication I received a letter from a concerned reader who made it clear he felt that the verbal is the faith and that our actions do not count.

His was a thoughtful position; for the Scripture does say, "Because if you confess with your lips that Jesus is Lord and believe in your heart that God raised him from the dead, you will be saved" (Romans 10:9). But I could not accept the idea that actions are of no importance.

In a second letter the reader went on to say that being saved is a "once in a lifetime" event and that nothing that happens afterward has any effect on the ultimate destiny of a Christian. Even if a Christian committed robbery, adultery, or murder, it would not be a factor in God's judgment of him or her. We used to call such a doctrine "Once in grace, always in grace."

However, generations of believers, even those who claim "once in grace," have been concerned with moral issues and have felt that behavior does matter. Many biblical passages warn us that our salvation is not complete until we have kept the faith and lived the life.

In this lesson we will examine such a passage.

FAITHFUL LIVING

Apparently, some of the early Christians interpreted the new freedom that Paul talked about in a way that permitted them to do whatever they wished—as long as they said they had faith. Paul practically accuses them of deliberately sinning in order to see how much grace God will bestow to counteract the sin. He asks, "Should we continue in sin in order that grace may abound?" (Romans 6:1).

The apostle quickly answers his own question. "By no means! How can we who died to sin go on living in it?" (Romans 6:2). While the Christian is free of the ceremonial laws, there is no freedom for immorality or license. Such attitudes and behaviors are inappropriate to the new life in Christ, just as they were to the old covenant. Sins are still acts to be avoided, dangers to be fought.

Paul maintains that justification has cleared the decks of a Christian's past sins; these are no longer held against the faithful. But he has no sympathy for the notion that Christians are therefore free to do anything. Sin is still sin. Morality is still morality. God expects the best of those who claim the promise.

In Galatians, written shortly before Romans, Paul has already said, "Live by the Spirit, I say, and do not gratify the desires of the flesh" (Galatians 5:16). Paul means more than sexuality when he speaks of "flesh": "fornication, impurity, licentious-ness, idolatry, sorcery, enmities, strife, jealousy, anger, quarrels, dissensions, factions, envy, drunkenness, carousing, and things like these" (Galatians 5:19-21).

It seems certain that to Paul, sin was both singular and plural, both sin and sins—not just a basic condition, but specific acts. And it covered a lot more than just sexual acts; a variety of other attitudes and actions was included. Clearly, continuing those actions and attitudes is not compatible with the life of faith.

What effect does the new life in Christ have on sinful behavior?

Walk in Newness of Life

Paul understands that the Christian is a changed person. This change is variously called the "new life," "life in the spirit," "a new being," "a new creation." Christians are the "chosen of God," those "ordained for adoption." In them is a new power and a new mind.

Yet they must learn to walk in newness of life and to deny the claims of the old self, which never completely depart. Paul acknowledged that there was a war within him. He often did not do what he knew he ought to do and did do what he knew he should not do (Romans 7:14-25). The only solution for those who follow Jesus is to "set their minds on the things of the Spirit" (Romans 8:5). The demands of "the flesh" must be rejected. A conscious decision must be made to choose the good—conscious of God's act in Jesus Christ, conscious of the new life within us. But there is no automatic exclusion from the results of sin, and the battle is not won until we have endured to the end.

Our abiding hope is that God is a merciful God and that those who love God will also love the people of God, even when they fail to be perfect in all things.

How does your Christian faith help you to resist sin?

United in Life and Death

The glory of the cross is that sin no longer has dominion over us. Sin is resistible and curable because Jesus has conquered both sin and death by the Resurrection. Sin, which once could only be balanced by acts of sacrifice, may now be canceled by the grace of God. This includes not only past sins but also those that may occur after our new life begins. It is possible to be so "alive to God in Christ Jesus" (Romans 6:11) that our members will no longer be "instruments of wickedness" (Romans 6:13). We can expect to be strengthened by the power of the Spirit within us when we are tempted and to be forgiven by a loving God when we fail.

Therefore, although sin is still with us, it is no longer beyond control. Whether in life or in death, we are forever surrounded by the matchless love of God. Jesus' death on the cross is the guarantee that life need not be lived without spiritual resources and that death need hold no terrors. Even those who have failed can call upon the forgiveness of God and find the grace they need.

How does the knowledge that God is love help us cope with sin?

Sanctified Slaves

The word *sanctify* means "to make holy" or "to set apart." There is a connection between freedom from sin and "sanctification" (Romans 6:19), but there is some disagreement about the nature of the latter. Some claim sanctification is a result of the process of justification (or of the action of the Holy Spirit shortly thereafter). Others claim that it is a lifelong process that moves by holiness toward perfection.

Those who think that the holiness is instantaneous tend to downplay any continual effort to achieve oneness with God. Those who think of it as a process recommend devotional and practical steps for spiritual growth.

John Wesley, the founder of Methodism, understood sanctification as a process. He counseled "going on toward perfection" as the true goal of the Christian life. He felt that it might be possible to achieve perfection in this life but also understood that the accomplishment was less common than the effort. Wesley believed that so long as persons continue to grow in physical and spiritual maturity, they are doing what God wants them to do.

Paul seems to support Wesley's interpretation in Romans 6:19: "For just as you once presented your members as slaves to impurity and to greater and greater iniquity, so now present your members as slaves to righteousness for sanctification." Being a slave to righteousness is the opposite of being a slave to sin, and it is the precondition for personal holiness. The practice of right living is a path to sanctification; we may have to practice and practice before we arrive.

Yet there is a sense in which sanctification is with us from the beginning. We could not even hope to gain a life of holy living unless we were already made holy through the grace of God. The foundation for saying no to old ways of living and behaving and yes to new life in Christ is laid by justification and reconciliation. There is much of the new life still to be experienced, but the break with the old is possible only through the grace of God.

So we are slaves in search of sanctification. By becoming a "living sacrifice" (Romans 12:1), we enter the path of spiritual development that will lead to complete unity with God. That goal may not be fulfilled in this life, but it will be ultimately fulfilled if we continue in the way.

How has God's grace helped sanctify your life?

Instruments of Righteousness

We are called upon to become "instruments of righteousness" (Romans 6:13). While we know that sin is real and that we may fall into its trap without warning, we also know that we are capable of living holy lives. "The wages of sin is death, but the free gift of God is eternal life" (Romans 6:23). This lesson gives us insight into these resources for the new life in Christ:

(1) The grace of God, which brings us to justification, frees us from the burden of sin and brings reconciliation with God. In this new state there is power beyond any we have ever known. With this power we can face the temptations of life with assurance that we can overcome them.

(2) That same grace removes the power of sin to destroy our lives. Where once sin enslaved us, it now has become simply one more impediment of the old life to be faced and conquered. Even if we succumb, there is a loving, forgiving God whose desire is to make us joint heirs with Jesus Christ. The power of salvation continues as the strength of the holy life.

(3) Both the life of Jesus Christ and the Scripture he inspired serve as a guide for avoiding sin. The Gospels and the rest of the New Testament offer guidance, enabling us to set our sights on the best of life. Furthermore, Scripture assures us that when we do not know the way, we can count on God's patience and guidance as we search. Sanctification is prompted by the Spirit within us and commended in the Scripture before us.

(4) The resource of the Christian community is constantly around us. When the Christian community operates as it should, it helps us find the holy way, supports us when we falter, and rejoices with us in the victory.

Even in the midst of the reality of sin, we can become instruments of righteousness—with the help of God and our fellow Christians.

CLOSING PRAYER

Holy God, your presence makes us desire holiness; but our human nature calls us toward sin. Strengthen us, comfort us, and sanctify us. In the name of your Son we pray. Amen.

Chapter Five

SHARING
CHRIST'S GLORY

PURPOSE

To remind us that as children of God we share in the hope
of resurrection

BIBLE PASSAGE

Romans 8:9-17

9 But you are not in the flesh; you are in the Spirit, since
the Spirit of God dwells in you. Anyone who does not have
the Spirit of Christ does not belong to him. 10 But if Christ
is in you, though the body is dead because of sin, the Spirit
is life because of righteousness. 11 If the Spirit of him who
raised Jesus from the dead dwells in you, he who raised
Christ from the dead will give life to your mortal bodies also
through his Spirit that dwells in you.

12 So then, brothers and sisters, we are debtors, not to
the flesh, to live according to the flesh— 13 for if you live
according to the flesh, you will die; but if by the Spirit you
put to death the deeds of the body, you will live. 14 For all
who are led by the Spirit of God are children of God.
15 For you did not receive a spirit of slavery to fall back
into fear, but you have received a spirit of adoption. When
we cry, "Abba! Father!" 16 it is that very Spirit bearing wit-

ness with our spirit that we are children of God, 17 and if children, then heirs, heirs of God and joint heirs with Christ—if, in fact, we suffer with him so that we may also be glorified with him.

OUR NEED

It was a cold, dark, and blustery morning as we arrived at Main Street Church that Easter Sunday. Most of us older ones wanted to stay in the warmth of the sanctuary for the sunrise service, which the youth had planned months earlier. We protested that the bitter wind and blowing snow would make worship on the hill outside of town all but impossible.

The young people were adamant, however. They had planned an outdoor sunrise service, and they wanted it held on that hilltop. So we finally agreed, got in our cars, and drove to the foot of the hill.

As we climbed up the spiral cow paths to the crest, the good-natured grumbling continued, punctuated by sarcastic comments about comforting loving older adults. When we arrived at the summit, our worst fears were realized: It was very cold, and the wind on the top of the hill was much worse than in the valley. But we were there and ready for the service, so we began.

The Scriptures were read, our prayers were offered, and the special music was enjoyed. In the course of the service, the sun rose above the clouds, creating a breathtaking view of the snow-strewn countryside. By the time we came to the devotional message, the wind had receded and the warmth of the sun had permeated our bodies. The concluding litanies, prayers, and hymns rang across the valley; and there was joy on every face. We came away filled with awe, sensing that we had experienced an unforgettable time together.

Indeed, those who were present have not forgotten that morning. We still talk about it when we see one another. It was a little like the first Easter—when another group of persons went reluctantly about their duties and came away filled with wonder. Easter is always like that. The glory of the Resurrection never dims. Each time we celebrate it, we renew the joy that the women felt as they witnessed the empty tomb and heard the statement "He has been raised." We want to tell others the wonderful news.

FAITHFUL LIVING

No doubt the Resurrection was the catalyst that created the church. Without it the followers of Jesus might well have returned to their jobs and homes with only pleasant memories of inspirational times together. They were already in transit, fleeing the cross in despair. There is no evidence that any of them knew then the meaning of the Crucifixion, and their theology and ministry were yet to be discovered.

The Resurrection changed everything. The knowledge that Jesus lived again revived the flagging spirits of the disciples, and his appearances gave direction to their efforts. They learned what they were to do and how to go about it.

So the Resurrection is the central fact of the church. That is why we worship on Sunday instead of on Saturday, the sabbath of the Hebrew faith. The Resurrection allows us to look to the future with confidence.

Although many denominations pay little attention to Christian holy days and a few even consider liturgical calendars and special services an evidence of pagan influence, all of them observe Easter in some way at some time during the year. Christians everywhere know that to participate in the Easter worship service is to share in a glorious moment of salvation history.

What does the celebration of the Resurrection mean to you, personally?

Resurrection Freedom

As Paul dealt with the implications of the Resurrection, he saw clearly that a new era had dawned. The whole framework of human values was changed. Inspired by God, the apostle was able to give expression to this profound truth; and we are still extracting the meaning of his insights. Just as it took over 1500 years for the doctrine of justification by faith alone to emerge from the Scripture and to become the Protestant manifesto, so it has taken even longer for some of the other truths of the faith to be realized.

Easter is a reminder that we no longer live under the old laws or in the old environment (Romans 8:9-11). Paul spells it out by saying, "So then, brothers and sisters, we are debtors, not to the flesh, to live according to the flesh—for if you live according to the flesh, you will die; but if by the Spirit you put to death the deeds of the body, you will live" (Romans 8:12-13). This is an extraordinary passage; we must attend to its meaning carefully.

When Paul uses the word *flesh,* he means everything we mean by body: appetites, desires, appearances—in short, the material from which physical pleasures and ego satisfactions are derived.

If we are not debtors to the *flesh,* then we no longer owe any allegiance or honor to fleshly (material) things or processes. We are free both from the need to indulge ourselves and from the demands of those who would encourage our indulgences. We do not have to worry about whether we have luxurious homes or whether our lives are free of discomfort. We are not obligated to observe the economic conventions of religious holidays—times when we are expected to buy lavish gifts or fashionable clothing. Nor do we owe any debt to the providers. When threatened with the specter of economic ruin by those who object to restrictions on the manufacture or advertisement of pornography, gasoline-guzzling automobiles, tobacco, alcohol, or other drugs (Make your own list.), we do not have to be concerned. Nor need we be troubled by the complaints of those industries that exploit customers or workers; we do not owe them anything.

As Christians we are not the protectors of access to the pleasures of the flesh or of the economic fortunes of the world. We live in the Spirit. Our concern is to witness to spirituality. As we share in the hope of the Resurrection, we also share in Christ's glorious victory over the things of the flesh (materiality). Together, we can celebrate a new commitment to the things of the Spirit.

How do you feel about the use of Easter (or Christmas) as a celebration of material excess and/or an exhibition of finery?

The Spirit of Adoption

A news story told how children were swapped in a hospital nursery, and the error was not discovered for a number of years. When the mistake was realized, a strange thing happened. Both the children wanted to be with the same family. One claimed to be the victim of abuse while the other was happy where he was. It was suggested that both children be adopted by the preferred family. That way the legal relationship would be clear; and the children would live where they felt they would have the best care, no matter who actually sired and bore them.

The Resurrection placed the early church in a similar dilemma. Now that a new day had dawned, how were the Hebrews (the chosen people) who accepted Christ and the Gentiles who became Christians to relate to one another? Paul gave the right answer. The whole process reflects "the spirit of adoption." Living in the light of the Resurrection and being led by the Spirit, we are adopted into the family of God, whether we are Jews or Gentiles. We are now one family, fellow citizens of a common household, brothers and sisters of Jesus Christ.

This adoption means that we no longer have to endure the legalistic atmosphere of the old family structure, wasting time and effort with useless activities designed to win God's favor. It also means that we who were outside the chosen community are accepted as legitimate offspring. We are the children of grace, justified by faith and made one with all who love the Lord. Adoption is a positive expression, supporting the very best of both Jewish and Christian worlds. We do not have to give up our genetic origins in order to be inducted into the spiritual family of Christ that will nurture us all.

The death and resurrection of Jesus was the dividing line. Before that time, being saved was a laborious process, involving many rules and sacrificial acts. Afterward, it was (and is) a matter of grace, with God taking the initiative and the entire Christian family looking to the one divine Parent. All those who are led by the Spirit of God have the hope of a more abundant life, in this world and beyond.

What do you value most about your adopted family in Christ?

The Spirit's Witness

The Christian community was founded upon the Resurrection, and every one of the early Christian writers laid stress upon the paramount importance of God's act in raising Christ from the dead. Paul, for example, repeatedly called attention to the Resurrection. He recounted the story in 1 Corinthians 15, relating what had happened and how many witnesses there were and why the event was of such importance to the Christian community. He also talked about the resurrection body and its imperishable nature.

The Christian doctrine of the Resurrection was not like the Greek notion of immortality, although Paul points out that they do have some apparent similarity. Persons will live forever with the Lord, not because they are naturally immortal, but because they are resurrected with Christ. It is Jesus' resurrection alone that assures all those who live in Christ that they will have life everlasting.

But how do we know we are part of that group? What signs are given to the believer confirming that justification has taken place and that he or she has been reconciled to God? No vote is taken. The body of believers cannot determine whether a person is a member of the household of faith. It is a matter between the believer and God alone. But how does one know?

The witness of the Spirit—that is how we know. "It is that very Spirit bearing witness with our spirit that we are children of God, and if children, then heirs, heirs of God and joint heirs with Christ—if, in fact, we suffer with him so that we may also be glorified with him" (Romans 8:16-17). God speaks to us through the Holy Spirit, the presence of God in the world since the ascension of Jesus. It is that inner voice that affirms we are accepted. Speaking to us in the recesses of our own heart and mind, it is the only confirmation we can have that we are redeemed and that we will be "glorified with him" (Romans 8:17).

How and when have you felt the Spirit's assurance that you are a child of God?

If We Suffer With Him

As he does with other words of reassurance, however, Paul quickly adds that resurrection glory will finally belong only to those who live with Christ through the whole of life. We do not join up for the short term; we do not get our reward just because we have our name on somebody's list.

Resurrection glory will belong to us if we endure the sufferings that are likely for those who serve the Lord. If we live with him in this life, if we can manage to hold on to our faith (and our sanity) even when it is not popular to do so, we will live with him forever. The power of the Resurrection is that which will enable us to do so.

Suffering for our faith may take many forms. For most of us in North America, it is not likely that such suffering will involve actual physical hardships. It is much more likely that suffering for our faith will result from subtle psychological assaults by those who want us to give lip service to the faith but to adopt practices that deny its validity—for example, employers who insist that profits are more important than principle or friends who want us to join them in "the good life" at the expense of good morals. Suffering for our faith can even result from the efforts of some fellow "Christians" who want us to join in their prejudices against persons of different appearance or belief and who attempt to shame us if we do not.

We need to remind ourselves that it was the suffering that gave meaning to the Resurrection. The cross preceded the empty tomb. And so it may be in our lives.

What strengthens you in times of suffering with Christ?

CLOSING PRAYER

You who set the Resurrection before us as a sign of your love, set now before us our calling so that we may serve you and thus live with you. In the name of Jesus Christ our Lord, we pray. Amen.

Chapter Six

LIVING IN
THE SPIRIT

PURPOSE
To contrast living in the flesh and living in the Spirit

BIBLE PASSAGE
Romans 8:1-11

1 There is therefore now no condemnation for those who are in Christ Jesus. 2 For the law of the Spirit of life in Christ Jesus has set you free from the law of sin and of death. 3 For God has done what the law, weakened by the flesh, could not do: by sending his own Son in the likeness of sinful flesh, and to deal with sin, he condemned sin in the flesh, 4 so that the just requirement of the law might be fulfilled in us, who walk not according to the flesh but according to the Spirit. 5 For those who live according to the flesh set their minds on the things of the flesh, but those who live according to the Spirit set their minds on the things of the Spirit. 6 To set the mind on the flesh is death, but to set the mind on the Spirit is life and peace. 7 For this reason the mind that is set on the flesh is hostile to God; it does not submit to God's law—indeed it cannot, 8 and those who are in the flesh cannot please God.

9 But you are not in the flesh; you are in the Spirit, since

the Spirit of God dwells in you. Anyone who does not have the Spirit of Christ does not belong to him. 10 But if Christ is in you, though the body is dead because of sin, the Spirit is life because of righteousness. 11 If the Spirit of him who raised Jesus from the dead dwells in you, he who raised Christ from the dead will give life to your mortal bodies also through his Spirit that dwells in you.

CORE VERSE

The law of the Spirit of life in Christ Jesus has set you free from the law of sin and of death.   *(Romans 8:2)*

OUR NEED

A passing reference has already been made to Henry Scougal, the seventeenth-century Scottish Presbyterian mystic who wrote of the life of God in the soul of human beings. Generations of Christians, have found him a source of great inspiration. In a quotation from his most famous book, we can see how he described living in the Spirit:

> It is now time to return to the consideration of that divine life whereof I was discoursing before, that "life which is hid with Christ in God". . . .
>
> As the animal life consisteth in that narrow and confined love which is terminated in a man's self, and in his propension toward those things that are pleasing to nature; so the divine life stands in a universal and unbounded affection, and in the mastery over our natural inclinations, that they may never be able to betray us to those things which we know to be blamable. The root of the divine life is faith; the chief branches are love to God, charity to man, purity and humility. . . . Faith hath the same place in the divine life, which sense hath in the natural, being indeed nothing else but a kind of sense or feeling persuasion of spiritual things.[1]

Even in the archaic English of this version, the point of emphasis clearly stands out. The origin of the life in the Spirit is faith, about which we have spoken extensively in previous lessons; and its evidences are love toward both God and human beings, purity, and humility. We will examine these evidences in conjunction with our printed biblical text in this lesson.

FAITHFUL LIVING

Someone has described the tendency of many of us to use psychological terms we hardly understand as "psychobabble." In that spirit we sometimes speak of a "compulsive personality," by which we usually mean anyone who is very interested in some activity that does not interest us. But there are compulsions that cause some of us to do things we cannot explain. They drive us to wash our hands twenty times a day or to blink our eyes rapidly when we are nervous or to shoplift items we do not need.

Perhaps it is some sort of compulsion that Paul has in mind when he contrasts living in the flesh and living in the Spirit. "Those who live according to the flesh set their minds on the things of the flesh," he says in Romans 8:5. That is, they are obsessed by physical and material concerns. They are constantly involved in tending to their material desires or seeking out their personal advancement.

They could be said to have a compulsion to win at any cost, to buy expensive possessions, to have illicit sex, to pick fights with people, to start cliques, or to react with envy to every accomplishment or advancement of their neighbors. If this seems an inaccurate description, just read how Paul describes these people in Galatians 5:19-21. Surprising, isn't it?

It could almost be said that those who are set on the flesh feel a compulsion to evil. They often are unwilling to recognize that what they do is wrong. They think of it as healthy competition or natural behavior or harmless fun. At times, each of us may feel a similar attraction, which is why the Scripture tells us always to be on our guard.

"To set the mind on the flesh is death" (Romans 8:6), Paul warns. In this passage he probably means the loss of the spiritual life instead of the pain of physical death. We all know that sinners do not necessarily die before the rest of us, but Paul claims that they never really live at all. They are dead to the true life, the fullness of life in the Spirit. Whatever punishment may await them in the hereafter, Paul is concerned to explain that they are also missing the best of life here and now.

How do you combat the urge to seek satisfaction of personal desires at the expense of the fullness of spiritual life?

Christian Compulsion

Paul also describes life in the Spirit as governed by strong urges: "Those who live according to the Spirit set their minds on the things of the Spirit" (Romans 8:5). Just as the person who is in the flesh is driven by the things of the flesh, so the one who is in the Spirit is motivated by the things of the Spirit. Just what are "things of the Spirit"?

The Galatians passage we cited to gain some understanding of the nature of the flesh is followed by an account of the results of the action of the Spirit in people: "By contrast, the fruit of the Spirit is love, joy, peace, patience, kindness, generosity, faithfulness, gentleness, and self-control. There is no law against such things" (Galatians 5:22-23). Notice how the list refers to characteristics people are to display in the social settings of their everyday worlds rather than to qualities they might develop in the cloisters of their spiritual retreats.

Some people do seem to have a compulsion to pursue the fruits of the Spirit. In our present parlance we often call such folks "do gooders" or "bleeding hearts." Of course, we also have men and women who like to spend time in prayer and personal devotion. We tend to approve of the latter group because they do not obviously interfere with our own lifestyles. Still, we do not want even these persons to get carried away. We tend to become much more suspicious of those who are "too religious" than of those who are not religious enough. We call the compulsions of the flesh "just human nature," but we call the compulsions of the Spirit "rigid piosity" and dismiss them as the preoccupations of fanatics. Odd, isn't it?

We do occasionally have persons who claim that the crimes they commit are caused by a spiritual experience. In a television interview, the killer of John Lennon (a member of The Beatles singing group) said that God told him to do it. Such occasional aberrations make us wary of "religious nuts," and we sometimes use these aberrations as a reason to distrust genuinely spiritual individuals. But the real reason many of us do not like those who are spiritually motivated is that they make us feel so uncomfortable with our own lives. These people remind us that we are not living in the fullness of the Spirit ourselves.

How would you define the difference between a religious fanatic and a person living in the Spirit?

Characteristics of True Life

Since Paul addressed the matter of the spiritual life (life in the Spirit) many times, we are able to identify numerous characteristics that he highlighted. None of them is sufficient by itself to define what life in the Spirit means; but taken together they give a portrait of the true life, the life lived in the fullness of the Spirit.

The words of Henry Scougal in relating the "branches" of the divine life give us a starting place. One of the characteristics of life in the Spirit is that it is filled with love for God. While God does not require our love in order to justify us, we will naturally love God as a result of our understanding of the way grace works. "God's love has been poured into our hearts," we read in Romans 5:5. It is only as the divine love comes to us in grace that we can love God as we should.

Following the order of Jesus himself, Scougal identified the second branch as charity to humans. When he uses the word *charity*, he means love in its broadest sense. "What can be more noble and generous than a heart enlarged to embrace the whole world?"[2] he says.

Paul speaks in the same terms: "Let love be genuine; hate what is evil, hold fast to what is good; love one another with mutual affection; outdo one another in showing honor" (Romans 12:9-10). Or, as in Romans 13:8, "Owe no one anything, except to love one another; for the one who loves another has fulfilled the law." There is nothing that betrays the shallowness of the claim to spiritual insight more than a failure to express and maintain love toward other human beings.

The third branch of life in the Spirit is purity. So much has been said about that in previous lessons that it hardly needs further emphasis. It is simply impossible to maintain a vital spirituality in the absence of a personal commitment to the virtuous life.

Scougal's fourth branch is humility, which is most difficult to define and keep. We are repeatedly warned against pride: "I say to everyone among you not to think of yourself more highly than you ought to think" (Romans 12:3), as well as, "For if those who are nothing think they are something, they deceive themselves" (Galatians 6:3). Jesus taught humility, and every writer of the New Testament echoes his concern. Humility is a primary Christian virtue, a radical commitment to honesty about one's status and accomplishments.

However, even if we have given up all pride in worldly things, we can easily develop pride in our "spiritual" knowledge or actions. Spiritual pride is even worse in some ways. The Letter to the Colossians points out how damaging people who think they "know it all" about spirituality can be. "Therefore do not let anyone condemn you in matters of food and drink or of observing festivals, new moons, or sabbaths. . . . Do not let anyone disqualify you, insisting on self-abasement and worship of angels, dwelling on visions, puffed up without cause by a human way of thinking" (Colossians 2:16, 18).

How many times have we heard people expound on how regular they are with sabbath observance or speak of visions they have had or mention how much they have given up for the Lord or declare that they have guardian angels? That is dangerous stuff. Only by "holding fast to the head," Jesus Christ (Colossians 2:19), can we be sure that we are seeking his glory and not our own.

What are some additional characteristics of the spiritual life?

More About Life in the Spirit

From the Letter to the Romans and from other letters in the New Testament, we can add to our list of marks or characteristics of life in the Spirit.

From the text of this lesson and from sources in other Pauline letters, we know that one of the characteristics of this divine life is peace. Abiding in peace with one another is one of the expectations of those who live in Christ. Contentiousness and factionalism are condemned; and, of course, the disposition to peace can be extended to the whole world.

Another characteristic is tolerance. Regarding those who differ from us or who commit some error, Paul counsels gentleness and patience in such situations; that is, he counsels the response of our Lord. Jesus told the disciples that they need not punish persons who went about witnessing differently, for there were other sheep in a different fold. We have different gifts, and we need to be free to express them—and to free others to express theirs.

Righteousness is another one of the marks of the life in the Spirit. Righteousness means not only observing personal moral requirements but also expressing justice and mercy in interpersonal relationships. Respecting the majesty of God means respecting the dignity of others as well. People living in the Spirit keep justice for all in mind. They practice equal treatment and seek to free those who are bound by injustice.

In summary, being in the Spirit means that we actively seek the good. In the closing words of his letter to the church at Philippi, Paul says, "Finally, beloved, whatever is true, whatever is honorable, whatever is just, whatever is pure, whatever is pleasing, whatever is commendable, if there is any excellence and if there is anything worthy of praise, think about these things" (Philippians 4:8).

What a comprehensive statement that is! It involves us far beyond what is normally considered the routine of religious life. It means that beauty and truth and honesty and artistic merit and excellence in all things are legitimate concerns of all who live in the Spirit. In the Sermon on the Mount, Jesus said, "Is not life more than food, and the body more than clothing?" (Matthew 6:25). True human life is—and in the Spirit we have gained such life, such abundant life.

Take stock: How well do you measure up to the standard of life in the Spirit?

A Final Note

Whenever we talk about life in the Spirit, we do not mean a part of human life or a part of God called the Holy Spirit. We mean all of life and all of God. We use the term *Holy Spirit* only to identify the presence of God in the world, not to differentiate among the activities of God. So when we say—or Paul says—"life in the Spirit" or "being in the Spirit" or

"God's Spirit dwelling in you" or "Christ in you," we really mean life infused with God's gracious power. That is what God has offered us, and that is what we seek.

[1]From *The Life of God in the Soul of Man*, by Henry Scougal (Sprinkle Publications, 1986); pages 45–46.
[2]From *The Life of God in the Soul of Man*; page 74.

CLOSING PRAYER
God of all life, Spirit of abundant life, fill our lives with the fruits of your Spirit. In Jesus' name we pray. Amen.

Chapter Seven

USING GIFTS TO SERVE

PURPOSE

To help us appreciate and make use of the diversity of gifts of ministry within the body of Christ

BIBLE PASSAGE

Romans 12:1-18

1 I appeal to you therefore, brothers and sisters, by the mercies of God, to present your bodies as a living sacrifice, holy and acceptable to God, which is your spiritual worship. 2 Do not be conformed to this world, but be transformed by the renewing of your minds, so that you may discern what is the will of God—what is good and acceptable and perfect.

3 For by the grace given to me I say to everyone among you not to think of yourself more highly than you ought to think, but to think with sober judgment, each according to the measure of faith that God has assigned. 4 For as in one body we have many members, and not all the members have the same function, 5 so we, who are many, are one body in Christ, and individually we are members one of another. 6 We have gifts that differ according to the grace given to us: prophecy, in proportion to faith; 7 ministry, in ministering; the teacher, in teaching; 8 the exhorter, in

exhortation; the giver, in generosity; the leader, in diligence; the compassionate, in cheerfulness.

9 Let love be genuine; hate what is evil, hold fast to what is good; 10 love one another with mutual affection; outdo one another in showing honor. 11 Do not lag in zeal, be ardent in spirit, serve the Lord. 12 Rejoice in hope, be patient in suffering, persevere in prayer. 13 Contribute to the needs of the saints; extend hospitality to strangers.

14 Bless those who persecute you; bless and do not curse them. 15 Rejoice with those who rejoice, weep with those who weep. 16 Live in harmony with one another; do not be haughty, but associate with the lowly; do not claim to be wiser than you are. 17 Do not repay anyone evil for evil, but take thought for what is noble in the sight of all. 18 If at all possible, so far as it depends on you, live peaceably with all.

CORE VERSE
We have gifts that differ according to the grace given to us.
(Romans 12:6)

OUR NEED

To introduce this lesson on gifts, here is a "test." Take a few minutes to read all the items. Then put a check beside those you feel you do well:

(1) Explaining things to people
(2) Telling others about the faith
(3) Tending to people's needs
(4) Helping people understand each other
(5) Communicating in dramatic ways
(6) Taking charge when needed
(7) Understanding the meaning of things
(8) Making people feel cared for
(9) Giving graciously

(10) Speaking before groups
(11) Making unusual things happen
(12) Identifying religious frauds
(13) Encouraging and supporting others
(14) Gathering and using information
(15) Listening and/or acting sympathetically
(16) Helping people toward health
(17) Maintaining calm in times of stress
(18) Arranging meetings and programs

Now, match the numbers you have checked with this list of gifts, based on 1 Corinthians 12, Ephesians 4, and the text from Romans:

(1) Teaching
(2) Evangelism
(3) Serving
(4) Interpretation
(5) Tongues
(6) Leadership
(7) Wisdom
(8) Pastoring
(9) Giving
(10) Preaching/prophecy
(11) Miracles
(12) Discernment
(13) Encouragement
(14) Knowledge
(15) Kindness
(16) Healing
(17) Faith
(18) Managing[1]

This way of looking at gifts is designed to help us understand that there are many gifts, not all of them mysterious.

Several involve things we do all the time. This lesson will look more closely at the meaning and use of gifts.

FAITHFUL LIVING

Paul's first mention of gifts is in the First Letter to the Corinthians. He wrote the letter after people from the Christian community in Corinth sent messengers with some practical questions for him about the new faith. There were inquiries about sex and marriage, about suing other Christians in civil courts, about the Lord's Supper, about morals, and about other topics. But the question on which Paul spent the most time was one about spirituality. As he implies in 1 Corinthians 12:1, the Corinthians wanted to know about "spiritual gifts."

While reading an older commentary (*The First Epistle of Paul to the Corinthians,* by Leon Morris, in the Tyndale Series [Wm. B. Eerdmans Publishing Co., 1958]; pages 166f), I found that the Greek word used in 1 Corinthians 12:1 is *Pneumatikos.* This word means something like "spiritual things" or "spirituality." From the rest of Chapters 12, 13, and 14 in First Corinthians, we can guess that the word was a term used in some congregations of the early church to refer to the ecstatic act of speaking in tongues. Paul states clearly that such euphoria does not prove the presence of the Holy Spirit; rather, confession that Jesus is Lord is the only criterion.

As soon as Paul has answered the question about *Pneumatikos,* he follows up with more about gifts. "There are varieties of gifts" (1 Corinthians 12:4), he says. This time, however, he uses a different Greek word, one that was not known outside the Christian community in the first century. The word is *charismata.* Paul was inspired in using this word; it is a Christian term with a specific meaning.

Since the Greek word *charis* means grace, *charismata* means "gifts of grace" or "gifts-in-grace." Paul seems to be advising the Corinthians not to worry about spiritual enthusiasms (*pneumatikos*) but to concentrate on the gifts of grace (*charismata*) God has given to build up the church. Gifts of grace, from the God who saves through grace—what a wonderful connection! This is a connection that we realize exists as scholars help us understand the original language of the text.

Paul refers often to the gifts of grace, always stressing their value and their variety. It could be said that the doctrine of the church set forth in Paul's letters is built upon the gifts of ministry (*charismata*) that come from the grace of God.

Why do you think Paul associated the gifts of ministry with grace?

Many Gifts—One Body

In our text from Romans, Paul begins by talking about sacrifice. One way to understand the phrase "present your bodies as a living sacrifice" (Romans 12:1) is to visualize the abilities we have been given by God (gifts) as being placed on the altar rather than our bodies themselves being so placed. This conception ties in very closely with the meaning and use of gifts of grace, for such gifts are God's way of equipping persons to do God's work in the world.

It is no accident that Paul moves from discussing sacrifice to talking about the body. From the very first, the gifts have been closely identified with the concept of the body of Christ or the one body in Christ. In both First Corinthians and Ephesians, the gifts are said to be for the purpose of "building up the body" (see especially Ephesians 4). In our passage from Romans, Paul puts it neatly together: "For as in one body we have many members, and not all the members have the same function, so we, who are many, are one body in Christ, and individually we are members one of another. We have gifts that differ according to the grace given to us" (Romans 12:4-6). (Note that the idea of grace is stressed again here.)

Why different gifts? From Ephesians we learn that we have different gifts because the body needs variety in order to "equip the saints for the work of ministry, for building up the body of Christ" (Ephesians 4:12). We have different gifts because it is necessary for the body's health and development that our gifts complement one another. That is, when each part works as it should, it "promotes the body's growth in building itself up in love" (Ephesians 4:16). We learn in 1 Corinthians 12:18-26 that even "the members of the body that seem to be weaker are indispensable" (1 Corinthians 12:22). The contribution of no person is to be ignored because "God has so arranged the body, giving the greater honor to the inferior member" (1 Corinthians 12:24). "God arranged the members in the body, each one of them, as he chose" (1 Corinthians 12:18).

No gift is of less value than any other, and every one is vital to the health of the body. So Christians are not to worry about whether other folks are thinking correctly or doing their part. Christians are to place their own gifts in the mix so that the body can be what it ought to be.

Moreover, the church or body can be said to be the sum of the gifts of its members. That means that no two churches are alike, just as no two bodies are precisely alike. Each congregation has a mission determined by the gifts that God has placed in its members. Discerning and embodying those gifts and that mission is what the church—or any part of it—is all about.

From what you know of the gifts of grace present in your group, what might be the task to which God is calling you as a group?

What Kinds of Gifts?

Whenever a group of persons talks about gifts of grace, someone is likely to say, "Well, I have never been able to see that I have any gift at all." Usually, the problem is that the speaker has never really understood what gifts of grace are. Studying the Scripture for this lesson can give us a better perspective on our gifts. There are several lists of gifts in the New Testament, including Romans 12:6-8, 1 Corinthians 12:8-11, Ephesians 4:11, and 1 Peter 4:10-11. Each of the lists includes some gifts not in the others.

Note also that different translations bring out different nuances of meaning. For instance, my favorite among the gifts is "encouragement" (Romans 12:8); but it does not appear in the New Revised Standard Version, which renders the word as "exhortation." However, both the *Good News Bible: The Bible in Today's English Version* and the New International Version translate it "encourage."

I draw two conclusions from these differences in the lists. First, the variety of gifts is much greater than the gifts included on all the biblical lists combined. What we have is only a sampler. Moreover, a person may have a version of a gift that is different from the versions other people have, making the possibilities for ministry even greater. Some gifts are dramatic, even exotic; but many are ordinary human traits, given by God for the good of the whole body.

Second, naming the gifts is not as important as using them. When we spend time arguing about the terminology, we lose the opportunity we have to carry out the ministry for which God has prepared us. Both Ephesians and First Corinthians say that each of us is gifted. That means that we all should be participating in the work of the church.

Using the test at the beginning of this lesson or some other guide, try to identify your own gift(s). How are you using it/them in the church?

Why Give People Gifts?

Our Protestant upbringing has led us to believe that any emphasis on working for the good of humankind may lead us into a dangerous "works theology." Since we are saved by faith alone, many of us get the idea that we are not obligated to do anything for the Kingdom except tell others about it. Many Protestants feel that way in spite of the story of the Last Judgment in Matthew 25:31-46, which emphasizes service and offers numerous reminders of tasks to be accomplished.

Paul's words in Ephesians 2:8-9 may give us a new insight about God's plan for the people of God. "For by grace you have been saved through faith," Paul says; "and this is not your own doing; it is the gift of God—not the result of works, so that no one may boast." But Paul adds a second sentence that many people miss: "For we are what he has made us, created in Christ Jesus for good works, which God prepared beforehand to be our way of life" (Ephesians 2:10).

So it appears that we are to do good works after all! But good works of a certain sort: those that God has prepared for us.

You may ask, "How did God prepare the works for us to do? Does each person have a predestined vocation? Or could it be that God has prepared us for the tasks of the Kingdom by endowing us with gifts that we are expected to use in whatever way will best serve the interests of those people God loves, which is all the people of the world?"

If that is true, then we need not fear a works theology at all. We are expert workpersons whose skills are essential to the grand plan of God: that all may come to know his love.

Considering the gifts you have, what kinds of "work" could you do for Christ?

What Sort of Environment?

As Paul does in every discussion of gifts of grace, he places the gifts under the auspices of love. His most famous passage on love, 1 Corinthians 13, excels all the others; but Paul consistently sets forth the truth that the capstone of gifts of grace is love. "Let love be genuine" (Romans 12:9), he says; for he knows that without it the gifts will not profit. The verses that close our printed Scripture spell out in more practical detail what works of love involve. In language that reminds us of the Sermon on the Mount, the apostle exhorts Christians to use our gifts for the benefit of others. Without love, gifts can become an occasion for competition as people seek God's attention or that of members of the congregation. Folks may spend their time posturing and bragging, usually claiming all the while that they are just "giving God the glory." But when gifts are used in the Spirit of the Giver, unity abounds and all grow in grace.

With love there is no hierarchy; everyone is talented in different ways. Whatever our occupation, whatever our office in the church, whatever our social position in the community, the worth of all is the same: We are children of God, saved by grace, called to use our gifts in grace for God and for others. All any of us has is the gift God has given, given to be offered in return.

"Love one another with mutual affection" (Romans 12:10), Paul counsels. Only in such a community of mutual love can there be a true church of Jesus Christ—a place where diverse gifts of ministry are appreciated and used.

[1] Slightly revised from *Each One a Minister*, by William J. Carter (Discipleship Resources, 1986); page 24.

CLOSING PRAYER
God of love, enable us so to respect one another that we may become one in sharing the gifts of grace you have given us. In the name of Jesus Christ, our Lord, we pray. Amen.

Chapter Eight

LIVING
FOR OTHERS

PURPOSE
To explore guidelines for responsible Christian living within the community of faith

BIBLE PASSAGE
Romans 14:7-19

7 We do not live to ourselves, and we do not die to ourselves. 8 If we live, we live to the Lord, and if we die, we die to the Lord; so then, whether we live or whether we die, we are the Lord's. 9 For to this end Christ died and lived again, so that he might be Lord of both the dead and the living.

10 Why do you pass judgment on your brother or sister? Or you, why do you despise your brother or sister? For we all stand before the judgment seat of God. 11 For it is written,

"As I live, says the Lord, every
knee shall bow to me,
and every tongue shall give
praise to God."

12 So then, each of us will be accountable to God.

13 Let us therefore no longer pass judgment on one

another, but resolve instead never to put a stumbling block or hindrance in the way of another. 14 I know and am persuaded in the Lord Jesus that nothing is unclean in itself; but it is unclean for anyone who thinks it unclean. 15 If your brother or sister is being injured by what you eat, you are no longer walking in love. Do not let what you eat cause the ruin of one for whom Christ died. 16 So do not let your good be spoken of as evil. 17 For the kingdom of God is not food and drink but righteousness and peace and joy in the Holy Spirit. 18 The one who thus serves Christ is acceptable to God and has human approval. 19 Let us then pursue what makes for peace and for mutual upbuilding.

CORE VERSE

Let us then pursue what makes for peace and for mutual upbuilding. *(Romans 14:19)*

OUR NEED

The late Albert C. Outler was an outstanding speaker and teacher. He could make people laugh about theology while they were learning it, which is no mean feat! In one of his lectures, which was later included in a book, he said this about John Wesley's view of the holy life:

In a hundred different ways, Wesley repeats the thesis: human unhappiness, in any and all its forms, comes from setting our love of creation above our love of the Creator, our love of self above our love of neighbor. But this is the generic definition of unholiness: innocent love corrupted by false loves. Thus he can argue that only the holy are truly happy, only the hallowed life is truly blessed, only the truly loving are actually joyful. The human potential is not self-fulfilling—and in any case it is bracketed by transience and death. All our truly human aspirations are self-transcending: they point to the love of God and neighbor as their true norms. But this is the essence of holiness. Inward holiness is, preeminently, our love of God, the love of God above all else and all else in God. Outward holiness is our consequent love of neighbor (all God's children, every accessible human being whom we may serve) with a love that springs from our love of God and that seeks the neighbor's well-being as the precondition of our proper self-love.[1]

Dr. Outler is suggesting that living a holy life has two foci: living for God and living for others. These emphases make up our theme for this lesson.

FAITHFUL LIVING

The story of Paul's involvement in the controversy over eating meat sacrificed to idols is a fascinating one. It began with Paul's trip to Jerusalem to attend the first general conference of the church, and it seems to have continued for the rest of his life.

The controversy itself started with a visit of some of the Judean Christian evangelists to Antioch in Syria. The church there had been first pastored by Barnabas, with Paul as an aide in the work of teaching (Acts 11:19-26). Although the congregation was predominantly Gentile in its membership, the Judean visitors maintained that all believers had to be circumcised, like the Jewish converts in Jerusalem. Paul and Barnabas tried to combat this outside influence with words; but the people from Judea insisted that they represented the real faith, the one Peter, James, and John presided over after the death of Jesus.

To resolve the impasse, Paul, Barnabas, and a few others were delegated to go to the headquarters of the church, which was in Jerusalem, to discuss the matter. Upon arriving, they met with the "apostles and the elders" (Acts 15:6), the power brokers. After a heated debate, Peter took the lead by saying that the Gentiles were proper subjects for evangelism and that it was not necessary for them to meet all the provisions of Jewish law. James (probably the brother of Jesus) agreed, with a few reservations. He suggested that the apostles and elders write a letter setting out basic conditions.

This letter did cancel the rule about circumcision; but it included the sentence, "For it has seemed good to the Holy Spirit and to us to impose on you no further burden than these essentials: that you abstain from what has been sacrificed to idols and from blood and from what is strangled and from fornication" (Acts 15:28-29). That these things were identified as "essentials" implies that they were very important to Peter, James, and other leaders of the early church. In addition, the reference to the Holy Spirit indicates that the authors of the letters were rooted in their faith.

When the emissaries returned to Antioch, there was great rejoicing. No one seemed to object to the conditions the apostles and elders had imposed. But Paul, apparently, did not completely accept the conditions.

What effect do you think differences of opinion had on the early church? How do such differences affect the church today?

Stop Judging!/Stop Eating!

When Paul identifies certain people as weak in faith, he singles out those who eat only vegetables (Romans 14:2). Their diet does not stem from some reason of health or moral concern. Rather, they avoid meat, believing it to be religiously unclean; for it may have been laid on the sacrificial altar of an idol. In voicing opposition to these people, Paul does not endorse consumption of meat from any source, however. His insight and sensitivity are much greater, much deeper.

What he actually says is that whether one eats meat or abstains is not the point. What is the point is that people must act from their own convictions to satisfy their own spiritual needs. It is not the business of those who think they are doing the right thing to accuse everybody who acts in a different way of being impious. But neither are those whose conscience is clear regarding a certain practice to act without concern for those with different scruples. Kindness and mutual respect are more important than judging between right and wrong actions and attitudes. So stop judging!

To understand the impact of Paul's words, we must remember that abstaining from eating meat sacrificed to idols was ranked equally with abstaining from fornication as an essential element of the faith by the Christian leaders at Jerusalem. These men also counseled not eating blood and not eating anything strangled, but Paul did not address those issues in Romans 14. He concentrated on the meat question because it gave him an opportunity to state a fundamental principle of Christian living: People are more important than impersonal rules or personal freedom. The focus of Christian life is neither the preservation of rules nor the protection of individual freedoms but the mutual fostering of growth in faith and discipleship.

Paul expresses his sympathy with those who are comfortable eating meat: "I know and am persuaded in the Lord Jesus that nothing is unclean in itself" (Romans 14:14). When they are alone or when they are with others who have no objections to the practice, it is apparently acceptable for those folks to eat meat that may have been offered to idols. But it is not acceptable to eat such meat when with someone whose feelings would be hurt by the action (Romans 14:15). So stop eating!

Of course, it is not fair to have our lives constrained by someone else's conscience (1 Corinthians 10:28-30); but it is not right to do something that undermines the values of another person. Paul wrote to the Corinthians, " 'All things are lawful' [including eating meat that had been offered in sacrifice to idols] . . . but not all things build up. Do not seek your own advantage, but that of the other" (1 Corinthians 10:23-24).

That is the heart of the matter. Everything that is done should be a help in maintaining good personal relationships. "Let us then pursue what makes for peace and for mutual upbuilding" (Romans 14:19).

How do you act when others behave in a way you find unacceptable?

Responsible Living

Paul also writes of the difference between those who value one day more than another and those who value all days alike. I have experienced that difference. Perhaps you have too.

Early in my ministry, a couple invited my family and me to their home for Sunday lunch. After we had Bible study and prayer, the woman left to put the food on the table. By the time she called us, I was starved. Imagine my surprise as I bit into the chicken breast to discover that the meat was stone cold! Also imagine my even greater surprise when I realized the green beans, the mashed potatoes, and even the biscuits and gravy were cold too, just out of the refrigerator!

Our hostess explained that she never cooked on the sabbath and that everything had been prepared the day before and stored for serving on Sunday. My personal feeling was that if a meal was going to be put in the refrigerator for the reasons she gave, it would have been better to offer ham and potato salad than biscuits and gravy. But I did not say anything.

Now, I knew that Sunday was not the original sabbath and that the woman had actually cooked the meal on the real sabbath, which is what we call Saturday. I also knew that Hebrew dietary laws do not apply to Christians and that all her efforts did not prove a thing—except that she was of a legalistic mind. But peace and mutual upbuilding are more important than correction of historical and theological errors, and peace and mutual upbuilding are usually accomplished through good manners. So I just ate my cold mashed potatoes as though I enjoyed them. (I did not, however, eat the cold biscuits and gravy. Manners only go so far!)

Paul recommends that we take the route of good manners every time we possibly can. There are times when somebody has to speak out, but those times are not nearly so frequent as we usually think. Even some of the things that we consider essential are not worth picking a fight about. If your brother or sister is not doing any harm to anyone, just try to live with him or her. To do so is to live responsibly.

Paul apparently feels quite strongly about the matter of peace and mutual upbuilding because he continues the theme in Romans 15:1-2: "We who are strong [or think we are, he might add] ought to put up with the failings of the weak, and not to please ourselves. Each of us must please our neighbor for the good purpose of building up the neighbor." There is that point again: Good personal relations are more conducive to spiritual growth than moral indignation is. If people are not mean spirited about their concerns, why confront them? For Paul that concept became a primary rule of life, one that could be applied in many places and situations.

What actions would you suggest a Christian ought to overlook? What actions require a Christian to draw the line?

Some General Principles

What can we conclude from Paul's comments on forbearance as related to differences about food sacrificed to idols and the observance of special days? Maybe you will draw different conclusions, but let me offer some of mine.

First, we need to understand that this is God's world, not

ours. We do not make the rules, God does. We do not even have to enforce them; God will.

Second, we are accountable to God, not to one another. Roman Catholics cannot hold United Methodists to their rules nor can United Methodists make Southern Baptists do what they consider right. Each must serve the Lord in his or her own way. After all, the Jew and the Greek both got in the theological door.

Third, not only all those television evangelists and peripatetic preachers (those who go around from place to place) but also we ordinary folks will have to learn that judging one another is not God's way for us. God's way is for us to love one another, even when we find it difficult or troubling to do so—perhaps most then.

Fourth, God does not really care how we dress the altar or how we sing the songs; but he does care whether we strive to build up one another in the faith. Decorate and sing for praise to God, not to meet some rules. There are not any rules anyway, except those that facilitate our worship together. We may each worship differently and still revere the same God.

Fifth, the primary Christian standard is love. It is better to be wrong about the proper order for Holy Communion than to be wrong about love. Love is the Christian form of communion with God and with others.

Sixth, there is less to worry about than we think. It is amazing how many traditions and environments have produced great Christians—even some who behaved rather oddly, like Francis of Assisi. But weren't they powerful?

Seventh, the doctrine of the gifts established that there is an almost infinite variety of ways Christians can serve the Lord. There may be almost as many ways persons do not serve the Lord but are doing the best they can. We should lighten up. You never know how people may turn out. The Lord is patient. What about us?

Eighth, tolerance is a virtue, not a weakness.

Ninth, when the time comes to draw the line, let's be sure the line is in the right place. More importantly, let's be sure our hearts are in the right place too. That is the most important guideline for responsible Christian living within the community of faith.

What, if anything, bothers you about being tolerant with others? When have others been tolerant with you? Does mutual acceptance matter to you? Why or why not?

[1]From *Theology in the Wesleyan Spirit,* by Albert C. Outler (Discipleship Resources, 1975); pages 82–83.

CLOSING PRAYER
God of life, make us persons through whom your love can come into the world, building up others in faith and life. In Jesus' name we pray. Amen.